The Wild World of Grannies

The Wild World of Grannies

From Beginners to Intermediates

Anne Decalmer

© Anne Decalmer, 2008

First published 2008 by Munali Books

www.munalibooks.co.uk

anne.decalmer@munalibooks.co.uk

ISBN 978-0-9559458-0-9

Typeset in Lucida Bright 11.5/15

Illustrations and cover design © Ivana Svabic Cannon, 2008

Prepared by:
York Publishing Services Ltd
64 Hallfield Road
Layerthorpe
York YO31 7ZQ
Tel: 01904 431213
Website: www.yps-publishing.co.uk

To Tom and James and all my family

*Lurid tales of Granny's own experiences
will not be welcomed!!*

The surprise!

Son says, on the phone:

"Suggest you sit down, great news!"

No inkling. Not at all.

"Sally's pregnant."

Unexpected indeed, but truly a joy to the ears. Knitting, Moses baskets, gas and air, soft, pink toes - all running through expectant Granny's mind.

It is never too early to prepare for Granny-hood – you have about 7 months ...

*   Enrol in a keep-fit/yoga class immediately.

*   Buy a small set of dumb-bells to increase muscle and back power for baby carrying, cot lifting.

*   Train for the half-marathon or triathlon for stamina, this is quite insufficient but will help a little.

*   Acquire a thick-skin as soon as possible, you must expect extremely cutting remarks in the future from your darling. You will then learn not to wilt or cry when he utters, 'Granny, you've got a big bottom.'

*   Set aside an hour a day to study the art of folding nappies. Order your books from the local library on this topic.

*   Find a first aid course to enrol on straightaway. Granny will be so grateful when she is called upon to dislodge peas from her darling's nose, or eject lavender that darling has sniffed up from Granny's bowl of pot-pourri. Even worse, coping with a choking, turning blue darling.

*   Research – Granny must improve her mind and find out about the latest crazes and nonsense paranoid parents may be exposed to.

*   Seek out a course covering 'healthy cooking for fussy eaters'. Granny may be called upon to provide a meal with all the necessary vitamins and minerals considered essential by the paranoid parents.

NB: worms, woodlice, chips and sausages are very nutritious.

The dangers: rivalry between the two Grannies

Yes, sadly this may become a dramatic issue. 'Handbags at dawn' would be a happy resolution for the expectant parents and grandpas caught up in any feuding. Rivalry and even jealousy may begin to surface between the two competing Grannies very early on. Who will buy the pram, the cot...? Then after birth darling is amazingly tuned in at an early stage and soon detects a 'soft' Granny and exploits the need to be 'the *favourite* Granny'. This is when the fun starts.

Don't be an over-zealous prospective Granny

Understandably, Granny is very enthusiastic to buy items for her expected darling. Note this danger does not recede after birth. Granny must keep on the straight and narrow – she must come to terms with the fact that:

Darling will not need

33	Hand-knitted cardigans
3	Moses baskets
2	High chairs
4	Pushchairs/prams
2	Travel cots
1	Borrowed travel cot

An added twist is the Internet Freecycle Service now operating in many towns. Experienced mothers offer their unwanted baby items (junk) free of charge to any avid collector. This indeed is a frightening pitfall to an over-zealous Granny.

An unintended consequence will be a significant improvement in the profits of the local pub. Many Grandpas flee to their 'local' to avoid being swamped by a mountain of baby equipment and incessant discussion on little darling's needs.

Granny's silence over 'the birth'

Lurid tales of Granny's own experiences will not be welcomed over the intervening months so keep any gory details to yourself. Expectant parents will be scared enough already. *You* can still remember your experiences so clearly, but do not even whisper those ghastly words 'stirrups', 'tears & stitches' or being told to 'sit up and drain'. Even worse the picture you retain of your boobs being swathed in bandages to support the weight of your milk 'coming'. Prospective parents would probably only think they are 'old wives tales' and won't believe Granny anyway.

Granny has heard though that times have changed, no more shaving or enemas … Some improvements indeed.

Granny's best attributes

* Prozac-like calm.

* Dalai-Lama's sense of forgiveness.

* Good knee joints.

* A sense of fun – unflinching when wee'd over.

* No undue sensitivity to vomit or faeces.

* Highly developed selective deafness.

* Flexibility when dodging flying missiles.[1]

* Equilibrium at the sight of bogies, worms, dead woodlice, particularly when half-eaten.

* Ability to bluff when you do not understand – viz Moomins, Thomas the Tank Engine, incomprehensible discussions of complex playground games that defy explanation.

---

[1] *The urban myth about a Granny being blinded by a flying baby spoon is probably untrue but sets the tone.*

Watch out for 'other women' consoling or sympathising with Grandpa

Grandpa may be brought back to reality by a sympathetic land-lady who assures him that Granny will eventually remember that he *could* play a role in their darling's upbringing. However she warns him of the Three Day Rule – 'Grand-children, like fish, can go off after 3 days'.

Beware – an over-zealous Grandpa

Although less common the over-zealous Grandpa is most dangerous. After months of studied indifference a 'switch' may be thrown once little darling arrives. Grandpa has to be warned against adding to darling's collection of inappropriate toys. He must refrain from the manufacture of monster rocking horses, doll's houses, forts or railway stations of megalithic size. Working models of any projectile weapons e.g. trebuchets must either be completely vetoed or restricted to operation in the park when paranoid parents are not present.

Note: public liability insurance may be considered.

Family (dis) Harmony

The happiness of granny-hood can soon be eclipsed by family disharmony. Guard against upsetting new parents with your tried and tested common-sense ideas. Above all try not to react too visibly to their hare-brained modern parenting methods. The atmosphere can quickly become cloudy and lightning-charged.

Be willing to tolerate and even join in with -

Baby sign language.

Early potty training.

Washing

Amazingly a very contentious subject leading to terrible consequences in disharmony: to hand wash or use the delicate setting on the washing machine has been the source of many family schisms. How much liquid, powder, nappy sanitizer to use? One extreme example where Grandpa's method of washing everything at

60 degrees, maximum agitation, highest spin rotation resulted in a very shrunken and wrinkled Mummy Bunny. Her clothes were chewed up and unrecognisable, resulting in an inconsolable little darling and furious new parents.

A guaranteed way into New Parents Good Books

* Granny must turn up with a pre-prepared, organically-friendly, home-cooked dinner for the family.

* Provide several boxes of home-baked delights.

* On no account criticise, find fault, drop any unkind subtle hints, comment at all about new parents coping in their role as new parents.

* Be willing to help (only when asked) – to rock darling to sleep, sing soothing songs, bathe and dress darling.

* Be an energetic Granny – dig in the mud, crawl around the floor, read endless stories, join in darling's games.

* BEST OF ALL – don't hog darling: know when to vanish without fuss or delay so that new parents can spend time with *their* darling.

15

Re-usable nappies & the practice of origami

Despite their complex shape and Velcro fasteners re-usable modern nappies require extra padding for night-time absorption. The unsuspecting Granny will therefore be required to improve her nappy folding skills. Imagine an elongated, flattened kite shape – this must be reproduced exactly with a soft muslin cloth. Granny has to ignore her dithering, thumbs-only hands (later becoming even more difficult with heaving, kicking darling), while she constructs this perfect shape and slides it under her darling's squirming bottom. Then follows the outer nappy which has to be positioned correctly, finally the plastic wrap – truly a work of art. If Granny is successful with her origami she could be rewarded with a patient smile from onlookers who may not notice her body shaking from the stress.

Granny's essential rules for keeping the peace

Rule No 1:

Unless you are willing to join in too, don't waste your time by providing:

> coloured pencils, sharpener, paper & glue.

> sticker books, scissors.

> magic painting, brushes and water.

> boxes of toys and books.

Rule No 2:

Accept the fact that Granny will be asked to draw some unknown wood-wasp, double headed Farley steam locomotive or strange, recently discovered dinosaur. There may also be a need to cut out intricate patterns, do complex jigsaws without being allowed to look at the picture ...

Rule No 3:

Don't be surprised when great annoyance or impatience is shown at Granny's woeful shortcomings. Your darling's deep frown is a quelling sight for Granny – she is trying her hardest to master darling's latest computer game.

Rule No 4:

Delight in unexpected praise – this seldom happens, but wallow all the same. Your darling suddenly says, 'I'm very proud of you Granny'. The difficulties all seem worthwhile. Much more common is the biting retort: 'I'm *not* very proud of you Granny'.

Rule No 5:

Keep within arms-reach – a full tin of special biscuits, fruit juices, selection of fresh fruit.

Emergency Meal

Darling's favourite foods – small baking potatoes, sausages, Peter Bunny sauce, Whole Earth baked beans, granary bread, chocolate spread. (All organic – of course). Small baby crockery & cutlery. Plastic beaker/cup.

Tantrums

Inevitably Tantrums will occur. They are always traumatic but particularly hard to bear for Granny. When tired and aching from an exhausting day tantrums are bad news.

No amount of pleading or cajoling will work. The volume of shouts and screams will become so intense that they will drown any sound from Granny.

Examples

Darling is starving hungry, and wants dinner *now*. But the food needs to cool down. Your best-loved darling dives down on the stair carpet and tears into it, chewing madly. The decibels increase as blue carpet strands become embedded between small, white teeth. Granny must not laugh!

Easier to deal with perhaps is the breath-holding tantrum – although it can be rather alarming if your darling lies prostrate turning a darker shade of blue. [Eventually darling WILL breathe]. Granny may need to be adept at dealing with the frantic supermarket manager who is envisaging massive Public Liability claims.

Granny's brave face

Your sweet darling will undoubtedly come out with hurtful and unkind remarks which must be born stoically. Over a period of months you have struggled to knit a stylish jumper, encountering many re-works and unpickings. Perhaps the finished garment does look a little lop-sided but it is *full* of love. Granny waits expectantly but the cruel remark is soon flung out. The colour is boring and it itches too much because it feels too tight. Instantly discarded and forgotten. But Granny does remember all those hours …

Having endeavoured to follow darling's instructions in the art of drawing a weevil, a deprecating, scornful glance can wither Granny's confidence instantly. But she must not give way or show any sign. Smile bravely and offer to copy a cockroach instead from 'Fred's Encyclopaedia of Tropical Insects'.

How to keep your temper and cope with disappointment and frustration

Always keen to find stimulating activities for her darling, Granny has spent some time planning and searching for a new interest. Granny is a little nervous but anxious to start. However the unexpected could happen – *example:*

a. Granny has bought the wrong dinosaur and darling wants a different one.

b. Darling soon gets bored and wanders off.

c. Darling gets frustrated because Granny is doing most of it.

d. Darling wants to glue, paint and finish it all at once.

Granny has to accept the fact that the dinosaur idea was hopeless and might never get finished.

Granny's hidden smile

Be prepared to camouflage your smile quickly. Grandsons, even very young ones, are very preoccupied with their willies.

Granny has to ignore this as much as possible. She must remember that the prodding, pulling and digging at it is to be expected. Embarrassing questions too can be thrown out unexpectedly:

Your little darling asks, quite innocently 'Why hasn't Granny got a willy?' Granny has to have a skilful way of dealing with this. Perhaps it is a coward's way out. But remember that to burst into a nursery rhyme or a funny song, perhaps to point out a spider on the ceiling may do the trick.

Granny's dirty jobs

A practised Granny will protect little darling from paranoid parents who may become hysterical over quite minor things. She will do this by keeping extremely vigilant throughout the day and become accustomed to swiftly wiping melted Jaffa cakes from the electric-barred fire, cleaning up half eaten pears tucked at the back of the sofa, smeared chocolate wiped onto bathroom towels, rescuing Mummy Bunny from the toilet bowl, washing her and getting her dry for night-time. Most important of all perhaps, locating as soon as possible, any poo that has dropped out of a nappy while Granny was changing her darling. Paranoid parent had already stepped in one dollop only recently in bare feet, leaving Granny feeling riddled with guilt.

Cunning Granny

Granny will eventually need to become a little cunning and devious at times while keeping a calm exterior. Granny must conceal items of contraband food in her pocket at a moment's notice. She must never leave her darling's half gnawed sweetie bars or disapproved items of food around the house to be spotted by snoop-eyed paranoid parents. All wrappings and 'give-aways' must be discarded immediately, any tell tale drips from munched blackberries or smeared chocolate from her darling's face or clothes wiped clean before being spied on. *NB* – crisp fragments can be a particular hazard

A well-practised Granny won't feel any compunction at discarding pairs of muddy socks in the dustbin after an unscheduled visit to the park, simply because she forgot darling's wellies. This saves paranoid parent heartache and Granny from detection.

To spoil or not to spoil, that is the question

Try and steel yourself against spoiling your darling. It is so easy to fall into the trap. To quell paranoid parent's furious glance at yet another purchase for darling explain that you found the gift in your local charity shop. The counterfeit sticky label showing 'Oxfam-50p' will prove your point.

Granny has to be strong and decide when enough really is enough, even though darling is having great fun. She must draw the line severely when she finds darling scrubbing around the toilet seat with paranoid parent's toothbrush.

Granny's Sensible Golden Rule

If you want to get away with it, *do it* as rapidly as possible.

Example: sprinkle grated chocolate on darling's cereal while paranoid parent is having a lie-in. Unfortunately this Golden Rule can only be relied upon before darling has mastered speech.

Granny's tough exterior

Darling will probably have an uncanny knack of causing great physical pain unexpectedly. Granny must acquire a 'second sense' early on, otherwise she must not be surprised at losing a tooth or contact lens in a matter of seconds. She must remember long-forgotten skills such as side-stepping adroitly from darling's cannoning head aimed at her knee-cap. The secret is to look for a tell-tale gleam in her darling's eye and purposeful stagger that can turn into a GBH head-butt or the gentle stroking that develops into a vicious slap.

When retiring for bed after a long hard day, she must not worry if she notices several purple weals and bruises on her arms and legs, knowing that in time they will gradually fade. Occasionally when darling cuddles up to Granny and says, 'I love you, Granny', tears of love well up and all agonising moments are forgotten.

Essential Words of Warning - Food

Granny must always remember that young children have delicate digestive systems and that vomiting can often be projectile.

One ample bosomed Granny given to displaying a generous cleavage received a deluge of half-digested salmon and broccoli into a position where she firmly declared only her husband's hands had ever been before. She then needed to borrow a pair of her son's jeans and shirt to get home in some semblance of respectability.

Coping with embarrassing remarks

To excel at being a 'Marvellous Granny' constant practice is required at diverting unfortunate remarks which come from darling's lips when in company, shops or at playgroups.

Examples:

a. 'Gran-*ny*, my scrota is itching.' Darling offers an obvious, somewhat annoyed explanation for his scratching, while Granny smiles lovingly, trying not to shrink away from horrified stares.

b. 'Granny, why has that lady got a big bum(p)?' Question asked at local swimming pool when observing a heavily pregnant lady in her swimsuit.

Granny must appear unruffled and steadfast in her thoughts and reactions answering quickly and sensibly to stem those persistent questions. Divert little darling by offering favourite sweets, ice-cream or other *forbidden* treats.

A well-trained Granny will not:

a. Wear pastel coloured, up to the minute, expensive designer clothes.

b. Have manicured, highly polished nails.

c. Be obsessed with maintaining her own appearance or dignity.

A well-trained Grandpa will:

a. Change nappies and (preferably having washed hands) cook edible meals.

b. Kick a ball about and go on death-slide with granddaughter.

c. AND even submit to dressing up clothes and fluorescent nail paint!

But they both will:

a. Have psychic powers to enable them to interpret certain cries, signs from darling or paranoid parent.

b. Expect to be totally knackered by the end of the day.

Ending seriously

Never forget that 'your' darling is not really *your own* darling. The parents are ultimately responsible, however inept they seem to be! You may not agree with or approve of their hare-brained methods or rules but you must appear to respect their wishes, even though they seem crazy to you. You are treading on very thin ice when you suggest alternatives – so be devious.

YOUR NOTES

What Worked

What you got away with

Disasters – and when you were found out